After the Revival

After the Revival

Carrie Jerrell

WAYWISER

First published in 2009 by

THE WAYWISER PRESS

14 Lyncroft Gardens, Ewell, Surrey KT17 1UR, UK
P.O. Box 6205, Baltimore, MD 21206, USA
http://waywiser-press.com

Editor-in-Chief
Philip Hoy

Senior American Editor
Joseph Harrison

Associate Editors
Clive Watkins   Greg Williamson

A CIP catalogue record for this book is available from the British Library

ISBN 978-1-904130-38-3

Printed and bound by
T J International Ltd., Padstow, Cornwall PL28 8RW, UK

for my family

Acknowledgements

Grateful acknowledgment is made to the editors of the following publications in which these poems previously appeared, sometimes in different form:

32 Poems: "When the Rider Is Truth."
Best New Poets 2005: "When the Rider Is Truth." (reprinted)
Birmingham Poetry Review: "Bill Moore Removes Leeches from My Legs after I Ignore His Advice and Walk My Kayak Ashore through Leaf Cover," "The Poet Prays to the 9mm under the Driver's Seat," "Tennessee Snapshot," "When the Rider Is Hope"
Cadence of Hooves: A Celebration of Horses: "Mustangs."
DIAGRAM: "The Dollar Dance," "Love Letter Written While Speeding Past the City Limit Sign" (published as "Drive"), "View of Petersburg from Bell's Hill Strip Mine, Pike County, Indiana."
Eleventh Muse: "Plainsong."
The Formalist: "The Processional."
Harbinger: "I Am Thinking of My First Horse."
Iron Horse Literary Review: "Love Letter Written While Watching a Hawk above the Petersburg, Texas Cemetery."
Image: "The Fire Tower," "In an Indiana County Thick with Copperheads."
Painted Bride Quarterly: "The Getaway."
Passages North: "The Poet Prays to Her Radio for a Country Song," "Demolition Derby," "For the Sparrows Who Lost Their Nests in the Southern Indiana Tornado," "The Recessional."
Rhyming Poems: A Contemporary Anthology: "The Bouquet Toss."
Sonnets: 150 Contemporary Sonnets: "The Processional" (reprinted), "The Ring."
Sewanee Theological Review: "Self-Portrait of the Artist as Glezen, Indiana," "What Goes Around."
Subtropics: "Big Daddy."

"The Bridesmaid," "The Chicken Dance," "The Groom's Cake," and "The Invitation" appeared in the tinyside *Four Weddings and a Mirror* from Big Game Books.

Thanks also to my friends, teachers, and fellow students for their faithful criticism and encouragement along the way, particularly Bill Baer, John Hollander, John Poch, Mary Jo Salter, Dave Smith, Bill Wenthe, and Greg Williamson. Thanks to everyone at Waywiser, and to Alan Shapiro. Many, many thanks and much love to the gang at Sewanee. Last, I am eternally grateful to my family, especially my parents, Brooke, and Matthew, for everything.

Contents

Foreword by Alan Shapiro   11

The Poet Prays to Her Radio for a Country Song   15

I

Demolition Derby   19
For the Sparrows Who Lost Their Nests in the Southern
    Indiana Tornado   20
Nocturne   22
The Country-Western Singer's Ex-Wife, Sober in Mendocino
    County, California   23
Tennessee Snapshot   25
Self-Portrait of the Artist as Glezen, Indiana   26
View of Petersburg from Bell's Hill Strip Mine, Pike County,
    Indiana   27
Plainsong   28
Love Letter Written While Watching a Hawk above the
    Petersburg, Texas Cemetery   29
Love Letter Written While Speeding Past the City Limit Sign   31
The Poet Prays to the 9mm under the Driver's Seat   32
Big Daddy   33

II

The Processional   37
The Ring   38
The Invitation   39
The Dress   40
The Veil   41
The Unity Candle   42
The Bridesmaid   43

Contents

The Father of the Bride   44
The Officiant   45
The Best Man   46
The Maid of Honor   47
The Bouquet Toss   48
The Garter Toss   49
The Cake   50
The Groom's Cake   51
The Dollar Dance   52
The Chicken Dance   53
The Getaway   54
The Recessional   55
The Toast   56

III

When the Rider Is Hope   59
I Am Thinking of My First Horse   60
The Fire Tower   61
Dogmata   63
What Goes Around   65
In an Indiana County Thick with Copperheads   68
When the Rider Is Pride   69
Mustangs   70
Bill Moore Removes Leeches from My Legs after I Ignore His
    Advice and Walk My Kayak Ashore through Leaf Cover   71
After the Revival   72
When the Rider Is Truth   74

Index of Titles and First Lines   75
A Note about the Anthony Hecht Poetry Prize   78
A Note about the Author   79

Foreword by Alan Shapiro

Imagine that Dolly Parton and Phillip Larkin had had a child, in or out of wedlock, and you'll have some idea of the poet you'll encounter in the pages of Carrie Jerrell's *After the Revival*. Jerrell's voice assimilates and transforms the most attractive and accomplished qualities of Parton and Larkin into something sassy, wise and wholly her own. Hers is a world of small town preachers, coal miners, prom queens, trailer parks, Kwik-N-Ezy's, honky tonks and road trips with either gospel or country-western music playing always on the radio. Hers is also a world rich in the metrical and musical traditions of English and American poetry, of sonnets and sestinas, blank verse and free verse, and of the gritty idioms of American speech.

Like Larkin she writes unflinchingly about romantic love, and the disappointment, self-deception and betrayal that love so often leads to. She knows "real life has no respect for fairytales," but like Parton, she can't stop singing as if it did. Like Parton, too, she is drawn to mystery at the same time that, like Larkin, she has no tolerance for mystification. She resembles both poets, moreover, in having a pitch perfect ear for the high and low occasion, for the wedding ceremony and the one-night stand.

While pain of one kind or another informs nearly all her poems, there is nothing but radiant energy to be found on every page of this marvelous book. Jerrell brings a wild exuberance to the world and everything in it, an exuberance "that's two parts sex and one part scripture, / that wears work boots to wardrobe / on opening night and when handed pink chiffon / says, *Baby, you know I don't do delicate*." She sings about despair with a transfiguring wit. Like the handgun she addresses in "The Poet Prays to the 9mm under the Driver's Seat," she has "a way with wounds."

Carrie Jerrell is a poised, mature and brilliant poet. Her distinctive genius, what makes her unlike anybody else I know, is her ability to bring together such a heterogeneous mix of worlds and influences – to be open to everything formal and informal, profane and sacred, foreign and home grown. If she wanted to, she could write with equal power about King Kong or King Lear. In her impurity, which in my view is another name for inclusiveness and generosity, she is a quintessentially American poet. *After the Revival* is like a great song: once you hear it, you can't forget it. This is a book you'll want to know by heart.

I run to death, and death meets me as fast

– John Donne

Oh my my, Oh hell yes,
Honey, put on that party dress.
Buy me a drink, sing me a song,
Take me as I come 'cause I can't stay long.

– Tom Petty

The Poet Prays to Her Radio for a Country Song

O guardian of the well-lunged, purveyor of lies,
enabler of the backseat horny, I am sorely afflicted.
Traveling the long tongue of highway 40,
I fear the bottomless black sky of loneliness
has hawked me from the back of its throat
and doomed me to land, wet and without notice,
in the dust-bitten spittoon of Oklahoma.

Have mercy, and do not leave me in my despair
to the size two pop star's manufactured vibrato
or my own heavy static. I confess I drive
a foreign make. I refuse to use home color
on my hair, and once again I've let heartbreak
put his hands in my back pockets. How I need
a song tonight – the kind that's all curves,
that's two parts sex and one part scripture,
that wears work boots to wardrobe
on opening night and when handed pink chiffon
says, *Baby, you know I don't do delicate.*

Descend, you blue jean honky-tonk angels,
and play my pain in 4/4 time on fiddle and red
birdseye-aproned steel guitar. Let my voice be open
as a screen door, all latchless and breeze-blown,
all invitation. May it reach like a revival choir
my man standing by the entrance, and may he tug
at his collar from the heat. Minor spirit,
I have been blinded by love's late night hallelujahs,
but I hear the blue notes coming. I've had enough
measures of introduction. Let me testify.

I

Demolition Derby

His '89 Impala ran four minutes
before two tires blew and I became
the candy stuck in a steel piñata, shitless
scared but falling for the spinouts,
the gut punch of the rush, the airbrushed flames.
I learned from him how to bend with broadside hits
and when caught in the metal's grip to get unhooked.
I didn't mind smashed fingers, the busted lip,
or blues the morning after, the smell of cooked
rubber in my curls and his bent-fender
smile at the breakfast table. These days I strip
the cars myself, a singular contender,
unable to shake off that first race, that boy,
winking as he strapped me in and sent me chasing
more than just a crush. I need a ploy,
a partner, a tempered alloy to keep from placing
last in every heat, but behind are wide,
deep ruts from spinning endless figure eights,
double-clutching, and flashing the driver's side,
while in the grandstand crowd, the next man waits
to pick my pieces off this track where spattered mud
across my shirt dries hard and stains like blood.

For the Sparrows Who Lost Their Nests
in the Southern Indiana Tornado

After the F-4 drags its tail down rural route three
and the willow rests its disheveled head
on the newly shingled roof, my father calls me
to report debris: bike tires, sparrow nests,
the Jones' plastic swimming pool,
and one pink pocket-size New Testament.

Where I live in Texas, there are plains of sun.
I need a plastic pool. I need the Psalms.
I miss the Midwest hill and lake, red coonhounds
high on table scraps, the balm of honeysuckle
and rhubarb cake. But my home county's overrun
with tweakers cooking bathtub crank in houses
one dropped cigarette away from bursting
into flame. Their feathered neighbors watch
from holes in the ends of rusted clothesline poles.

House sparrows, white trash of the species,
when I fly home on my mother's prayer
with a pink swimsuit and a tin-can phone,
greet me at the door with your *cheep cheep*.
If I could buy you brick colonials set deep
in maple groves and safe from every spinning wind
I would, but all I've got are pocketfuls
of childhood fool's gold pecked from a gravel drive.
The trailer I grew up in sits alone, abandoned
at the edge of town like a whiskered old man
watching lightning from a busted lawn chair.
Ride out one last green sky and the poverty
of stars there with me, hunkered near
the bathroom plumbing, harmonizing
with the power line's hum, and singing
as if someone listened, as if we didn't need

For the Sparrows Who Lost Their Nests
in the Southern Indiana Tornado

two copper coins or the clothing of lilies,
as if we weren't trapped on cinder blocks, but free.

Nocturne

for Matthew

Twenty-two, come from the underground,
you're through with the mine's night shift and wear coal dust
like vernix while playing *Clair de Lune*. Moths crowd
the porch-lit screen door, and you've come to trust

your ear for every chord. Dark note by note,
how many hours you've searched for songs that burn
like lustrous rock – your damp neck creased with soot,
your hands unclean – only to be spurned

by stars repeating, *Time, Time, Time*.
My brother, in the pitch of sleep, may hymns
resolve for you. May dreams be more than ash.

May you climb to a house of blazing light and blind
yourself at its windows, breathe its music in,
and beat your wings like prayers against the mesh.

The Country-Western Singer's Ex-Wife,
Sober in Mendocino County, California

Somewhere back East my late love's all coked up,
another cowgirl wannabe lying
at his feet while he plucks a Willie Nelson song
from his beer-soaked six string and complains nobody
understands a rebel's broken heart.
I've played her part, the starstruck blonde in boots

and denim mini, boobs and brains to boot.
Whiskey-fed, dreamy, how I talked him up,
a sequined Tammy to his George, my heart
a backstage bed I wanted him to lie in.
It proved too hard, and when a harder body
came along, he said, *The party's over*,

and left me listening to "Sad Songs and Waltzes,"
Waylon, steel guitars that struck like a boot
to the face. But that's good country, right? A body
enamored with its bruises, praising its screw-ups,
the blood still wet in its wounds? Memory lies
as still as a rattlesnake until my heart

begs for its venom. *Sink 'em in,* my heart
says. *I've been traveling on a horse called Music,
and he's brought me here to die.* I'd be lying
if I said I didn't want to fill my ex's boots
with spit the night I caught him with that up-
start starlet at the bar; when everybody

tried to hide in their shot glasses; when nobody
but a Broadway street preacher had the heart
to hold my hair off my face while I threw up
outside; when all the songs I loved – "Crazy,"
"Golden Ring," "Jolene" – became like boots
too busted to put on, bent-pitch ballads of his lies,

The Country-Western Singer's Ex-Wife,
Sober in Mendocino County, California

my shame sung loud in the key of C. He's lying
from the stage, in the bar or bed, when he says nobody
understands him. I do. I've burned my boots,
moved west to wine and water because his heart
was a dry bottle, cold as the black rose
rotting in his lapel, and I still wake up

to his tunes: the beer, blow, boots and love, the lies
they tell and don't. Once, I was a good-hearted woman.
Now I pray, Lord, please, somebody, shut him up.

Tennessee Snapshot

There's a story goin' round ...
– Dottie West

Damp stacks of week-old *Southern Standards* slump
beside the Kwik-N-Ezy's door, where you
can purchase beer, live bait, and pork-n-beans
while "Sweet Thang" plays on ten-watt, blown-out tweeters.
I'm just outside McMinnville, Tennessee,
the home of Dottie West, the duet queen,
who told her stylist, *Tease it up to Jesus,*
and to whom, backstage at Tootsie's Orchid Lounge,
Ms Patsy "Fall to Pieces," "Crazy" Cline
said, *Hoss, if you can't do it with feeling, don't.*
Nobody belts a torch song like the dirt-
poor oldest girl of ten.
                              I hum along.
The glass door flashes my reflection: black
mascara running, wind-flattened hair, nails split
and bitten to the quick. I spread my Rand
McNally out across the T-bird's hood
as Willie Nelson sings the National Anthem.
In just six turns I could be in California,
but Dottie's house is only five blocks down,
and sitting on the wire, flashing her
white wingbars like rhinestones on a sunlit stage,
a mockingbird, state bird of Tennessee,
is covering the all-time greatest hits.

Self-Portrait of the Artist as Glezen, Indiana

I'm 4 a.m. deer-piss-drenched camouflage,
the haunted woods, the doe's brown eyes, the gun
and Tater Warner's hardware store on Main
and Cherry, baseballs aisle five, a tent
beyond revival, organ out of tune,
"Amazing Grace" played back-pew Baptist flat,
potluck to follow. Flying red-tail high,
I've circled every furrowed field for life
and only seen my shadow, the willow swing
by Panther Creek, an empty gravel road,
an unchained shepherd taking the long way home.

View of Petersburg from Bell's Hill Strip Mine, Pike County, Indiana

They've razed the Gospel Center where I crossed
my heart in water, died, and rose again.
There's been no county fair, no pageant queen
to take my crown and ride down all five blocks
of Main Street on the Fourth in someone else's
'67 Mustang, hot pink Dollar
General lipstick and a sequined dress
too short and rented out of town. The mines
are all shut down, land butchered like a cow.
At dusk, a thick mist settles on Bell's Hill
and summer sings "Oh Land of Rest, for Thee
I Sigh" on sluggish, D-flat minor winds.

This is where we'll bury it. River down,
crops withered, last good beef from winter eaten,
we'll lay one building at a time across
the bottom, shine empty storefront glass, repoint
the courthouse brick, and pray for forty days
of flooding rains until its streetlights glow
beneath the water like a second-rate
Atlantis, like the stars in dead reflection
off my eyes. You'll come like a witness then,
when the rest have left, and park top-down with your love
for fireworks bursting from some distant place.
I'll be here, whispering tall tales to boys
from out of state who'll put their hands where my heart
should be beneath my first-place sash, my skin
still coal-ash soft, legs tan and warm around them,
still strong enough to swim this pit and live.

Plainsong

If you saw my footprints around the barn loft's ladder,
you would know I tie each bale with sisal twine and secrets.

If you saw me kneel among cut sweetcorn stalks,
you would know I hear vespers in the auger's rush.

If Red-tails scouted the warren's edge, or murders called
from their barbed wire roosts, you would hide me in rows
of ruby snapdragons, mend my briar-lashed hands;

like the dobbin, you would carry me where jack-in-the-pulpits grow
beneath cathedraling white oak and hickory.

If sunset turned ripe wheatfields honey-gold,
and the combine hummed as it cleared the hundredth acre;
if, after dark, haze hung like a new heaven above the furrows,

you would know the harvest moon is near,
that sheets left on the line will smell of blazing stars in the morning,

and that I wait upstairs for you, barefoot on the pine floor,
unplaiting the amber linens of my hair.

Love Letter Written While Watching a Hawk above the Petersburg, Texas Cemetery

I'd been wishing for a river to rest beside
when you found me. I'd been pretending
my wish was a need. When you took me in,
I circled your bed, looking for something
to hold in my mouth: tuft of cotton,
pigeon feather, twig of a dead mesquite tree.
I thought I could call you home.
I thought I could build a nest.
When I said *love*, I meant *safety*.
When I said *safety*, I meant *please hold me down*,
so you bound me in the jesses of your arms
warm as leather. To prove I had no wings,
you floated the sheets above us, pressing
your palms to my back, but I rose on the air
to a pitch best measured in sighs, and you
and the ground disappeared below me.

This morning after rain, we followed hawks
to the graveyard overgrown, each plot
a miniature landscape I study: this one
with its loyal angels; this one with its wet
splintered cross; this one marked by a child's
dusty pinwheel. No matter how deeply I sink
my hands into these high mounds of earth,
my restlessness remains tough as a plastic daisy.
You think my heart is pretty like the angel's,
that my hair is prairie grass so long and quiet
it could be a kiss, but I know weeds from grass,
and the angels kneeling here are concrete.
Love, though your chest is the riverbed
I've hunted, and some nights I lie grave-still
beside you, I've always been more wind than root,
more weed than flower, and you should be
more wary of my shadow. I make a better hawk

Love Letter Written While Watching a Hawk
above the Petersburg, Texas Cemetery

than angel, and the same ground you break
between us I may bury you beneath.

Love Letter Written While Speeding
Past the City Limit Sign

Four summer months of third-shift factory eyes,
the half-assed hurdler's scabbed-up palms and knees,
the Levi's/flannel uniform, the prize
collection of Star Wars toys, the Pekingnese

next door you shaved for fun, the baritone
vibrato you'd start belting out to shut
me up mid-fight, the slice I gave your collarbone
the night you wrestled me and won. We cut

the Mustang loose on backroads liquid black,
the windows down, your hand on mine on the stick,
and somewhere in the rearview mirror's crack,
the fragments give a wicked view – the quick

blood rush, the touch, the bliss of skin on skin,
the thick dark hours of swollen heat, the thin.

The Poet Prays to the 9mm under the Driver's Seat

Coldest friend, pretty little monster,
I know relief lies low and left of center.

I'm looking for it now. The windshield
shines with my body's outline on its field

of nighttime glass, of stars on glass, though I'm
no star, just a waning mark at which to aim

my crooked sights. My days are all dry-fires,
and better actions call for calibers higher

than my own. Be savior to my lovesick bones,
groom to the primed bride of my loneliness,

and I'll forever be your best brief muse,
your straightest shooter. You have a way with wounds,

with damage and deliverance, and I make
a ready berm for both. Let your trigger's break

perform my lullaby. I'll hold the final note.
Bury it here, in the hollow of my throat.

Big Daddy

Called me Hot Stuff. Called me Ragtop,
Lugnut, your Deere-in-the-Driveway Duchess.

Called forth Bad Company from the pickup's stereo
and, lo, I appeared with a buck knife

and a hundred-proof smile, my battered hunter's manual
tucked in the waistband of my cutoffs.

What were we at first but two necks of the same guitar,
high on the blister of our power riff? Each night

was a stadium tour, each day an album cover
fit for collecting. How precious,

how practiced we looked those weekends at the lake,
posing in our matching hipwaders and stabbing

at the world's swamp-stink with the gig of our love.
But forever is a black fish hiding in cattails, a fat plop

always sounding out of range. Soon the lake iced over.
The far off smoke of forest fires stole your attention.

While I dreamt pyrotechnics for our stage duets,
you and your matchbox slid out the window.

No note. No final mix tape. No rose left thorny
on the nightstand. I searched for you in parking lots

until a passing trucker said he'd caught your show
in Denver, that you wore a silk shirt and played everything

Big Daddy

acoustic, and the news rocked me like a last track ballad.
Oh Big Daddy, Daddy with the Long Legs,

father of a stillborn promise and my liveliest rage,
for weeks I choked on your name, stuck so deep

in my craw it took a crowbar and two months
of keg stands in Assumption, Illinois to dislodge it.

Now, I drink sweet tea in a Southern state.
Now, I am patient. Small likenesses of you croak to me

from their lilypadded thrones. I'd like to mistake
their bellows for green apologies, but I know better.

At night, I hunt them with a three prong. I fry them
in batter and grease. We both know what they taste like.

II

Advise none to marry or to go to warre.

– George Herbert

The Processional

("Here Comes the Bride")

It comes from Wagner's opera *Lohengrin*,
when Elsa weds the knight whose identity
she swears she'll never ask. But mystery
is always overwhelming – the heroine
betrays their love to learn his name, and when
he disappears across the river, she
calls after him then dies in agony.

The congregation rises. Strings begin
to play. Out steps another Elsa, veiled
today from the truth that all love coexists
with death. She's just a momentary queen,
starting her own long walk from fairytale
first act to tragic final scene, who risks
them both for all the drama in between.

The Ring

These days, you don't just buy a solitaire.
You look for flaws with magnifying loupes,
check color grades, make setting choices: flared
four-prong cathedral, ridged contour, or flutes
of baguette accents down the sides. The bands,
once standard 14k gold, now come
in weapons-grade titanium. It stands
to reason, one would think, as rings become
unbreakable, the bonds they represent
might, too. But every master jeweler knows
about the unseen structural punishment
gems undergo, the blades, the saws, the blows
received on every face, the grinding hours
it takes for shapes like teardrops, hearts, and flowers.

The Invitation

On linen, laid, or vellum, deckle-edged
or damask bellybanded, engraved or blind-
embossed, it arrives and you, the privileged
announcee, learn from its Kate Spade design

the honor of your presence is requested
at yet another sentimental fête.
Like all the beer and buttercream you've ingested,
the St James script does nothing but sedate

your brain, except *and Guest*, two words you loathe –
an invitation to relive the pain
of every Wallflower Joe or Mystic-tanned

Don Juan you've brought who sweat clear through his clothes –
since there's no Mr to your Ms, just your name,
set down, alone, in someone else's hand.

[handwritten annotations:]

sarcasm

namebrand

bland except for "loathe"ing

loneliness / hollowness of the individual

invitation is Saks + stupidly fancy

The Dress

With its blush pink corset, crystal appliquéd
French lace, and satin bustle skirt beyond
your Cinderella dreams, it's Lhuillier,
six months of pay, a gown for *le beau monde*

that is, by midnight at your party, trash:
two chocolate handprints from your toddler niece,
stilettoed hemline holes, the ivory sash
Lambrusco-stained and smeared with prime rib grease.

Real life has no respect for fairytales,
their photo ops, glass shoes, and crystal carriage.
Worn down by the wicked truths that time unveils,
you'll soon forget them, too, and stuff your marriage

like one more of your cast-off couture frocks,
ill-fitting, yellow, and rotting in its box.

The Veil

At your final fitting, you think of Mexico,
the coming honeymoon, piña coladas
the size of football helmets, wine and tapas
by candlelight – anything but the slow
disintegration of your certainty
that he is *it*, the *one*, the *only*. You pull
the blusher down. It might as well be wool.
The boutique seamstress and your mom agree

it takes time to adjust. From where they sit,
you're flawless, but underneath your skin is crawling;
what about your in-laws? Secret debts?
And when did he start snoring? *Think sunsets, sex,*
ceviche in Los Cabos – the perfect trip,
if you make it down the aisle without falling.

The Unity Candle

One source reports it started with the Bible,
the man shall cleave to his wife (Genesis 2),
while others claim it's purely pagan, tribal,
straight from skirt-clad Scottish or Bantu

Sahara brides. More likely Luke and Laura,
soap TV's super-couple, are to blame.
They lit their flame for a first-rate crowd, an aura
of autumn sweeps about them, and proved a framed

assassin and her rapist could find bliss –
if only for a season. As viewers know,
scripts get revised, cast members change, the kiss

turns to betrayal, and love exists in flashbacks
where the past plays a killer cameo,
reciting promises as firm as wax.

downgrades, then comes back to the title

hollowness of marriage

tradition is fake & fancy

The Bridesmaid

Having played the roles of bride's best friend, groom's sister,
last minute fill-in, and token female cousin,
you're set for dyed-to-match high heels, the blister,
cold beef, warm beer, the chicken dance, and the dozen

well-meaning guests who pat your hand and ask,
Have you found someone special yet, sweetheart?
You've learned to include in the day's costume a mask,
a practiced smile and sigh to check your smart-

ass answer: what you've found are bantamweight
boy toys, e-freaks, sex pervs, and two prospects
who might have worked, had they not been mean or married.

What's special is the bubble bath that waits
at home, where a worn-out welcome mat bedecks
the threshold over which you won't be carried.

The Father of the Bride

When the tailor's club hand hovers near the crotch
of a penguin suit worth more than your last Winchester,
you remember, from that film your wife made you watch,
a line: *Armani don't make polyester.*

Now George Banks's meltdown in the grocery store
over four superfluous hot dog buns
(They're not ripping off this nitwit anymore!)
is a scene you understand: these wedding sons-

of-bitches make a mint off saps like you
who buy their daughters Beamers and Barbie dolls,
then La-Z-Boy along without a clue

until, armed with her best *You don't love me!* squalls,
she conducts another budget-busting coup,
your little girl, who's always had you by the balls.

The Officiant

Whether rabbi, bishop, reverend, or priest,
he's seen it all: pre-ceremony sex,
demonic flower girls, the crasher-ex,
and M.O.B.s as bitchy as the beast

of Revelation. He's entertained the crowd
(*Three popes walk into a bar ...*) while a no-show
bride fled town. He's endured Aunt Marg's solo
of "Ave Maria," and, *oy vey*, he's vowed

to quit – too many *chuppot* caught on fire
or couples tripping on the broom – but won't,
since the god he represents has yet to shove it.

Instead he smiles, cues the sinner's choir,
and blesses those who last and those who don't,
Shalom, ahuv, ahuvah, dearly beloved ...

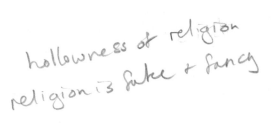

hollowness of religion
religion is fake + fancy

The Best Man

Spring Break with your Sig Ep brothers means blackjack
at Mirage, the Tropicana's topless show,
flaming cocktails at VooDoo Lounge, then back
to sleep it off poolside at Bellagio,

until one *frater*, Clooney-style, hooks up
with a Harrah's hostess – tattoo, belly ring,
implants, the works – and, oh, he's all shook up,
pawning his pledge pin for back alley bling

and dragging you to chapel, where he and his wait, er,
wife-to-be exchange their vows before God,
Elvis, and a stoned Priscilla impersonator.

You slap your brother's ass, get drunk, applaud
his moves, and turn a glazed eye to his mess
(just like old times), which is what you do best.

The Maid of Honor

As leader of your best friend's satin posse,
your duties include pre-photo makeup checks,
guarding the gifts, preventing the Triple-sec-
soaked in-laws from doing a risqué Bob Fosse

number on the table tops – a job
akin to that of foiling evil spirits,
like Roman maids first had. Here, evil rears its
ugly head in many ways: the poor slob

hoarding the hors d'oeuvres, the screaming kids,
and even, when your friend shows up months later
with a suitcase and a boutonnière-size bruise,

the groom. She's stunned, in danger, trapped on the skids,
and you're still playing the hero, the Mitigator,
a shield from trouble she does and does not choose.

The Bouquet Toss

On those occasions when you aren't able
to slip outside and smoke, hide in a stall,
or search just long enough beneath the table
for earrings that you didn't wear; when all
the girls press in as close as they can get,
you think of tip-offs, high school basketball,
your mother's scream, *Get on the floor for it!*

Maybe this time, despite the free-for-all
and since you know the bride (you're dating her brother),
you'll have a shot. She winks, then turns. You hold
your ground and watch the pass with a clear aim
at someone else sail past your reach, another
pathetic loss to some sixteen-year-old,
fresh, thin, and better built to play this game.

The Garter Toss

Way back in the 1300s, when girls were married
to rich French geezers at their fathers' whims,
bachelors considered gowns good luck and harried
poor brides for pieces ripped right off their hems.

But this ain't Medieval France – it's Jersey, baby:
men crowd your spot-lit chair while "Hot Legs" blares
from the DJ's booth. Your hubby's funds are shady.
Your daddy spent your teen years stoned downstairs,

and you were raised on Snoop, g-strings, and *Sex
in the City*. A modern *Cosmo* quiz whiz skilled
at Playmate poses, you perform this little striptease

like a pro: you hike your skirt. You flirt. You flex
your slender calves. You give these guys a thrill
and get your due – a husband on his knees.

The Cake

Your revelries as expert wedding crasher
(an out-of-town step-cousin of the bride's
masseuse) are all about Electric Slides,
hot guys, free booze, limbo, the occasional flasher,

and cake: white layers of classic buttercream,
exotic blood orange tortes, or charlottes iced
with spicy rum ganache, each singular slice
a confection of the couple's coupled dream –

which never included their top tiers being ganked
by a reject bride and stuffed inside her freezer,
though you believe they're rightful compensation

for the hopes your half-baked ex-fiancé tanked.
You keep each piece as an anniversary teaser,
a *what if*, self-served each night as consolation.

The Groom's Cake

Legend has it that if a single woman sleeps
with a piece of groom's cake under her pillow,
she will dream of her future husband.

Afraid to stifle its prophetic powers
with Tupperware or plastic wrap, you leave
it on a plate and tell yourself eight hours
alone with your Prince Charming, make believe
or not, is worth one ruined pillowcase.

But then you meet him. Balding, doughy, squat,
he's drinking Perrier at a NASCAR race.
Your first thought: *Where's Dale, Jr.?* Your second: *What*
if this comes true? You wave red flags at him –
your psycho ex, your O.C.D., your love
of Maker's Mark. He doesn't get the warning,
although to you these secrets serve as grim
reminders that you're sweet – just not enough,
the one mess you can't clean up in the morning.

Systemic
self-hate women
single women
are taught in our
culture.

The Dollar Dance

Once, you crashed a former flame's reception
and shelled out fifty bucks, to his wife's horror,
to make him squirm to Styx. For richer or poorer,
you rocked that party with your indiscretion
and found yourself blacklisted by every bride
in town as "bitch," "slut," "thug in three-inch heels" –
the stuff of beauty parlor legends. Appeals
made by your mother to apologize
(Sue Grady's son will never call you now!)
were met with looks as cold as frozen cake.
Five years and one fiancé later, you hope
you've been forgiven – could the crowd allow
you one dance for cash to Mr Big's "Just Take
My Heart"? Mom shakes her head and says, *Elope.*

The Chicken Dance

Bamberg, Germany, spring 2003:
your first reception with a polka band
and barmaids dressed in *kinderschuerze*. Free
from your latest lover, who couldn't understand

why kids weren't in your five-year plan (you're frugal,
and you've just lost 40 pounds), you're partnerless.
You just want someone to call you *Little Struedel*
for the night, but this crowd's low on loneliness:

the couples, families, drunk retirees
in *lederhosen* look so, well, so *happy* –
a foreign term – that soon their niceties
and steins of *Hefenwiesen* make you so sappy

you dance along in their squeeze-box poultry yard,
fearless for a moment, and flapping hard.

The Getaway

The work of bored, drunk groomsmen with twelve bars
of Days Inn soap adorns your supercab,
your V-8 Chevy, a local cruise-scene star.
Jacked up, tricked out, deep cherry with prefab
black racing stripes and Heartthrob twin exhaust,
she wears the name you gave her, *Little Lady,*
across her hip in bridal-white high gloss.

Now she's for sale (You bought a ring.), and Brady,
your best man and bachelor cousin, smears
his offer on your door, along with JUST HITCHED,
WEARING THE CHAINS, LET'S HOPE SHE'S NOT A LEMON.
You say you're trading up, but when you hear
those hollow High Life cans, you nearly kiss the ditch
on that long, last drive with both your favorite women.

The Recessional

(Mendelssohn's "Wedding March")

Applause.
          Then arm-in-arm they quickstep down
the aisle, matrimony's new recruits,
parading for the crowd of relatives
and seasoned friends who secretly count down
the days until the war begins: disputes
about which house, which job, which sedatives
will damp their A.D.H.D. kids; the sneak
attacks of Lust and Pride, the mind games played
by Insecurity, and Time's unending
siege leave so few survivors.
                    Lightning streaks
the sky. Children throw rice that ricochets
like buckshot off the car, and from impending
rain, the groom carries his bride so her train won't drag.
The wind unfurls it like a big white flag.

The Toast

May the road rise up to meet you ...

If life is a country and love a coast-to-coast
road trip, may your marriage be a Subaru,
a Bentley, a loaded Winnebago. Screw
the price of gas and gun it. Let rip a host

of victory burnouts and two-wheel all the curves.
Let solitary cyclists quake in their clips.
Let tailgaters curse your window's lipstick quips
(MONOGOMY IS SEXY!). You'll need nerves

as steely as a Skylark hood when hail
pummels the windshield or dust storms wipe the road
from sight, but stay with the vehicle. In time,

you'll own a classic beauty the rest will trail
forever, jealous of your view: a rainbowed
horizon, clear lanes, and one last hill to climb.

III

When the Rider Is Hope

We pilot evening's cryptic air
fused as faith and plea in prayer.
My burden's to become pure flight;
his, to right me if I scare.

When my blind spot blurs the fence,
he imparts his confidence:
his *Easy girl,* his loose-rein hands,
reprimand my reticence.

Heel to rib, approach then thrust,
I'm suspended by his trust,
playing earth's brief renegade
in bascules made of breath and dust.

I Am Thinking of My First Horse

after Teresa Ballard

A dun, his body the only kingdom
I know the whole of. His cheek broader
than the shoulder blade he rubs it against,
my shoulder blade. I braid his hair
like my hair: mine, the color of sweet feed;
his, night river black. I bathe his saddle marks,
cinch marks, bridle sores, though I cannot
give him back his body unbroken,
the way I have been promised mine
in heaven. Because each morning the world
nuzzles me awake; because my breath
and sunlight and the wind-lashed shadows
of branches outside my window form
a tangled braid of tributaries I will one day
ride to a river dark as a horse's eye;
because I imagine he waits on the bank
to carry me, I am thinking of my first horse,
how we will leave our scars in the water
behind us, entering a kingdom we praise
but cannot ever fully know.
I am thinking of my first horse
because I want no heaven without him.

The Fire Tower

I

Eight, mouthy, and proud, you didn't want his help,
so while you watched the stairs revolve below
your feet with every gust, your father watched
you climb the last three flights dizzy, on your hands
and knees, before your brother, crouched by the door,
jumped out to scare you, and you missed the step.
Which felt worse, time's yawn as you went down
or air across your bit-through lip, you don't
remember, but you slapped him, hard, and sent
his paper airplanes to the ground in shreds,
holding your hollow apology until
his wails ran through the summer trees like flames.

II

At sixteen, you climbed there with your first. Shed shoes,
dress, slip that disappeared down so many flights
of darkness, wearing your sweat in beaded stars
across your collarbone, a universe
you wanted him to rule. Next day in church,
you lied about the bruises from your fall.
When your turn came to answer Heidelberg,
What does the law of God require of us?
you stretched your skirt across your knees and passed.

III

From the office window on the sixteenth floor,
you think trees circling the hospital
seem predatory in their brilliant orange.

Your doctor holds the model DNA
as he explains the flaw in your design,
your treatment options, how much time you have.
The double helix turns, a spiral stair,
in you from the start, sending you back
to see it one last time, aging, condemned,
the first steps broken. You recall the climb
of Luther up Rome's Scala Sancta, raw-kneed,
steps kissed with Pater Nosters, how he asked,
And yet, who knows if this is true? You know
that posture, practiced since you dreamt yourself
alone in the tower, waving handkerchiefs
of pages torn from a book that didn't end.
And even though your legs can't carry you
to the top, the picture of what's waiting there
is clear: the autumn blaze, spray-painted hearts,
initials scratched like undeciphered codes,
your name somewhere among them, rusting away.

Dogmata

Something about the lone
gas station's windows that night,
the traveler thought,
approximated the divine:

the efferent bullet holes,
light spreading its splintered beauty
onto the parking lot.

So terrible then to find
that a simple wave of the hand

or her body's mass
before the wounded glass
could make the beams
change shape, disappear.

And what of the prices,
posted and high, for a broken
pump and the shelf's stale wafers?

The cashier shrugged,
and the skin of his cigarette
pulled back from the ash.

A skewed crucifix,
the station's sign burned
in her mirrors. She drove,

watched instead a red dawn
and the needle's extraordinary fixture –
nothing left to move her

but hope, stuffed in the trunk
like the ransomed body of Christ.

What Goes Around

Vengeance is Mine ...
– Deuteronomy 32:35

You're leaving a city you never could call home,
cruising the concrete noose of its Outer Loop,
marveling that everything you own fits in your pick-up,
when you notice you're four exits past your exit.
You're in lane three of crowded six behind
a gravel truck, but the radio works. The tank is full.
In the next lane's beat-up Volvo, a couple gets lost
in a fit of operatic gestures. You can tell
by the way he jabs his finger in her face
and she smacks the dash with the flats of her hands
that they aren't singing with the music.
Caught looking, you catch a glimpse of something
you saw in yourself just last year when, still licking
your wounds, you told your ex's new girlfriend
a graphically embellished story concerning
his kidney stones; or further back, in college,
when you pulled a Delilah on your three-chord,
"rock star" boyfriend, leaving his locks to curl
like vipers on your vacated pillow; or your first time,
high school, sophomore year, when you
sweet-talked from the janitor the clubhouse keys
before the district finals, found the duffel
of the starting pitcher, and vaselined his jockstrap.

Revenge. *The big black pill*, your grandfather called it
from the pulpit, *and God alone should give out
the prescription*. Being born an addict and a thief,
you've known since your first stolen kiss
that Love's a dealer, too, sneaking those chalky caps
to every junkie's bang room, and after you give
her what she wants, she leaves one by the bed
in a standard issue, no-name envelope. Some flush it.
Others place it on their tongues for just a little taste.

You swallowed yours sans glass of water
or lightly buttered toast, stood before the mirror
as your eyes went black and practiced in your best
Jezebel voice, *Take him out and stone him to death.*

Of course, there was the coming down: the cotton-mouth,
the tremors, the sensation of plummeting like a bird
shot through with lead pellet and stripped of its beak,
the starved, green-eyed dogs pacing the street below.
And yet, someone always brought you back to life
to start it over, this cycle, beautiful and depraved,
orchestrated like all others by Time and his whirligig,
escapable only when the birthday top he sends you
finally stops its spinning. You wonder if you'll have
the habit kicked by then. God knows you're trying –
lopping off your hands, plucking out your eyes,
scolding your rearview reflection for being duped
this time by no one but yourself into thinking
you were more than just a playtoy – and although
this exodus is a necessary step toward your redemption,
it feels as damning as the fall behind it.

Broad is the way that leads to destruction!
your grandfather shouted before his altar calls,
the soloist primed and ready for a ten-minute
rendition of "Trust and Obey" to draw souls
down the narrow aisle. Once, on a dare,
you made the trip. When the deacons laid their hands
on you, praying for you a new, clean heart,
you figured you'd drop dead before you left the tent.
Instead, a dirty-blond boy drove you to the riverbank
where that fear, in the dark, revivifying whorl
of his warm mouth and water against your skin,
was sucked downstream, only to resurface at times like this,

on an asphalt sea, where the gum-patched vessel
of your pride founders. You stare at the woman
in the Volvo staring back, and the string wound round
your heart pulls so tightly you nearly roll
your window down to tell her if she wants
to spin that steering column like a wheel
of fortune, go right ahead – you understand.
Except it's not your place. That's here, lane three,
behind the gravel truck with its loose tarp
like a giant hand that's knuckleballing back
every stone you ever threw, where even though
you can't see your exit sign, you know it's up ahead,
as sure as sin, glowing green in the high-noon sun,
just waiting for you to come on back around.

In an Indiana County Thick with Copperheads

Tweaked out on her mother's meth,
the twelve-year-old walks
the county roads of my childhood,
sees stars in a sky crow-feather black,
finds the pack of wild dogs, the teeth
of the mottled Lab less frightening than
her uncle and his bristle-brush whiskers.
There's little left to do here but grow
long and mean, to meet each day
like a belly meets gravel. In church,
the sleepless preacher says, *Our sins
and snakes are many. The Lord is still
displeased.* He prays, thunders like Moses
for deliverance and a penny serpent
for the Judgment Day. Next door,
the slap of the father's hand against
his son cracks like lightning,
and the weed they grow between
Blue Angel hostas feeds off their storm.
I've tried to escape this place –
like the horses, I can sense what's hiding
in the tack room, curled behind
the ancient plow or wrapped around
the whips – but it's my beginning,
and I haven't found the end.
I tell myself Moses was a murderer
forgiven, that snakes only strike
when threatened, but when I go to the river
to relive my baptism, and my flesh is buoyed
by water, the gold strands of my hair
darken and dart out with the current,
as though they have lives of their own.

When the Rider Is Pride

In sudden veils of sleet, on ice-skimmed stone,
the only name he whispers is his own.
His heart could fit inside my coffin bone.

Mustangs

You camp along the deep Cheyenne,
the Lakota's sacred river flowing in all
four cardinal directions so summer-slow
you think it's made of tar or crude oil dreams
you can't wade through. You're thirsty
as Crooks Mountain, waiting for mustangs
from the northern plains to cross here,
split into two herds, one moving to the thick interior
of western pines, the other to the east,
through high canyons where they'll graze
in landscapes grand and lavender. You want to stand
in that split, stretch your arms in both
directions, so you wait, skin cracking
like the Badlands under the golden sun.
Your rations gone, the hunger rings in you,
a pain so hollow you could play it like a flute
except your mouth is filled with sand,
not song, so you keep waiting,
drag yourself to the river's shallow bed
but see no reflection through the silt. You kneel
there. You have finally forgotten your name.
The ground shudders, but before you see them,
you hear the slow code of their pounding hooves
build in you like a cresting wave, your eyes
fixed on the ridge they'll shadow,
and you know you'd wait forever here
for their wind to cool your neck, for one clean look
into the wet mirror of a dark eye,
one chance to ride
bareback, thighs trembling at the strain,
a specter flashing through the raw Black Hills,
your hands knit like music and air,
inextricably, in a white mare's mane.

Bill Moore Removes Leeches from My Legs after I Ignore His Advice and Walk My Kayak Ashore through Leaf Cover

What you don't hear when I wade out are the *shits*
whispered as not to offend you, preacher,
kayak guide, friend. But you know. I pray the richer
red of river silt accepts my blood as penance.

Pain is part of Adam's curse, you say when I wince;
the rest is death and I'm a fallen creature
like my first father. You're a patient teacher,
not scaring me with that. As one who commits

a pet sin knowing that it damns, a leech
behind my knee twitches with joy before
you pull it off, bring a stone down on it. *I'm sorry*,

I say. We learn from shame, its silent itch,
as I did when you gripped me with such force
and wrenched from my flesh what drank my life with glory.

After the Revival

We gather at the river in our polyester blends.
We gather in our sunburnt skins,
sore from the daylong sermon, a bright
congregation of frailties. To my right,
a man cleans his trifocals with his shirtfront.
To my left, a woman taps her titanium knee,
says, *It'll outlast me*. From weed
and willow edging the bank, the vellum
whir of yellowjackets stirs my hand
to touch three scars from childhood stings
along my jaw, three scars from the day
of my baptism, three stings as I stood
by the river, my throat swelling and swelling
until I dropped to my knees in the clearing,
my hair still wet when my father at last laid
one hand on my shoulder, prayed,
Spare my daughter, then jammed the EpiPen
into my thigh. By which I was saved,
the plea or the needle, I can't say,
but before breath rattled its wings
behind my teeth again, I witnessed
the bunched velvet of thunderclouds
drag the distant ridgeline like a robe's
soiled trim across nails. My own Sinai,
my burning bush, I should have prophesied
but couldn't, too numb, unsure, and only twelve,
though the elders stood with their amens
poised around me. Since then, my throat's
been numbed by different means: horrors of love;
horrors of doubt; a sister's child laid to rest
in a wet grave; my father's stumbling
over stones in the fields he's plowed,
two black spots blooming in each of his eyes.
I've trusted too often the lens doctored

in chemical heat and not the eyes behind
my eyes, but this evening, after new humbling
and hymns tendered by failed voices, I see
that each willow leaf backlit by the apricot sun
is actually a candle set aglow and hovering.
My father stands there in invisible water,
blessing the baptized, his hands reading
their faces, and the air around him is quick
with thousands of wings. O Death,
so proud in your jacket of cheeriest yellow,
this world is a dark cloak I tire of wearing.
Take my eyes and hands. Take my throat
and the songs it traps, and I will still
remember those promises made in the shapes
of rivers. I am waiting for you here
on bended knees. Do not hide from me now.

When the Rider Is Truth

I am froth and lather, sent steaming
through jade fields while he sits
heavy in the saddle, beating love songs
on my flanks I'm slow to learn.
His snapped whip rings like church bells.
He prays my name. In different winds,
it rhymes with *win* and *race*. At night,
he rests against my neck and tells me
stars are born between my heartbeats,
though they're unreachable this trip.
Still, with him I feel sure-footed
running on this soil of sand,
this miraculous green,
where every day is like no other
in its symmetry of hill and valley.
When shadows blend, I want the blinders on.
I want the spurs and speed. It's then
I understand tight reins, the firm grip,
the bitter iron on my tongue,
the blood and sharper bit I'm driven with.

Index of Titles and First Lines

A dun, his body the only kingdom 60
Afraid to stifle its prophetic powers 51
After the F-4 drags its tail down rural route three 20
AFTER THE REVIVAL 72
Applause. 55
As leader of your best friend's satin posse, 47
At your final fitting, you think of Mexico, 41
Bamberg, Germany, spring 2003: 53
BIG DADDY 33
BILL MOORE REMOVES LEECHES FROM MY LEGS AFTER I IGNORE HIS
    ADVICE AND WALK MY KAYAK ASHORE THROUGH LEAF COVER 71
Called me Hot Stuff. Called me Ragtop, 33
Coldest friend, pretty little monster, 32
Damp stacks of week-old *Southern Standards* slump 25
DEMOLITION DERBY 19
DOGMATA 63
Eight, mouthy, and proud, you didn't want his help, 61
FOR THE SPARROWS WHO LOST THEIR NESTS IN THE SOUTHERN
    INDIANA TORNADO 20
Four summer months of third-shift factory eyes, 31
Having played the roles of bride's best friend, groom's sister, 43
His '89 Impala ran four minutes 19
I am froth and lather, sent steaming 74
I AM THINKING OF MY FIRST HORSE 60
I'd been wishing for a river to rest beside 29
I'm 4 a.m. deer-piss-drenched camouflage, 26
If life is a country and love a coast-to-coast 56
If you saw my footprints around the barn loft's ladder, 28
IN AN INDIANA COUNTY THICK WITH COPPERHEADS 68
In sudden veils of sleet, on ice-skimmed stone, 69
It comes from Wagner's opera *Lohengrin*, 37
LOVE LETTER WRITTEN WHILE SPEEDING PAST THE CITY LIMIT SIGN 31
LOVE LETTER WRITTEN WHILE WATCHING A HAWK ABOVE THE
    PETERSBURG, TEXAS CEMETERY 29

MUSTANGS   70
NOCTURNE   22
O guardian of the well-lunged, purveyor of lies,   15
On linen, laid, or vellum, deckle-edged   39
On those occasions when you aren't able   48
Once, you crashed a former flame's reception   52
One source reports it started with the Bible,   42
PLAINSONG   28
SELF-PORTRAIT OF THE ARTIST AS GLEZEN, INDIANA   26
Something about the lone   63
Somewhere back East my late love's all coked up,   23
Spring Break with your Sig Ep brothers means blackjack   46
TENNESSEE SNAPSHOT   25
THE BEST MAN   46
THE BOUQUET TOSS   48
THE BRIDESMAID   43
THE CAKE   50
THE CHICKEN DANCE   53
THE COUNTRY-WESTERN SINGER'S EX-WIFE, SOBER IN MENDOCINO
    COUNTY, CALIFORNIA   23
THE DOLLAR DANCE   52
THE DRESS   40
THE FATHER OF THE BRIDE   44
THE FIRE TOWER   61
THE GARTER TOSS   49
THE GETAWAY   54
THE GROOM'S CAKE   51
THE INVITATION   39
THE MAID OF HONOR   47
THE OFFICIANT   45
THE POET PRAYS TO HER RADIO FOR A COUNTRY SONG   15
THE POET PRAYS TO THE 9MM UNDER THE DRIVER'S SEAT   32
THE PROCESSIONAL   37
THE RECESSIONAL   55

THE RING	38
THE TOAST	56
THE UNITY CANDLE	42
THE VEIL	41
The work of bored, drunk groomsmen with twelve bars	54
These days, you don't just buy a solitaire.	38
They've razed the Gospel Center where I crossed	27
Tweaked out on her mother's meth,	68
Twenty-two, come from the underground	22
VIEW OF ST PETERSBURG FROM BELL'S HILL STRIP MINE, PIKE COUNTY,	
INDIANA	27
Way back in the 1300s, when girls were married	49
We gather at the river in our polyester blends.	72
We pilot evening's cryptic air	59
WHAT GOES AROUND	65
What you don't hear when I wade out are the *shits*	71
WHEN THE RIDER IS HOPE	59
WHEN THE RIDER IS PRIDE	69
WHEN THE RIDER IS TRUTH	74
When the tailor's club hand hovers near the crotch	44
Whether rabbi, bishop, reverend, or priest,	45
With its blush pink corset, crystal appliquéd	40
You camp along the deep Cheyenne,	70
You're leaving a city you never could call home,	65
Your revelries as expert wedding crasher	50

A Note About the Anthony Hecht Poetry Prize

The Anthony Hecht Poetry Prize was inaugurated in 2005 and is awarded on an annual basis to the best first or second collection of poems submitted.

2005
Judge: J. D. McClatchy
Winner: Morrie Creech, *Field Knowledge*

2006
Judge: Mary Jo Salter
Winner: Erica Dawson, *Big-Eyed Afraid*

2007
Judge: Richard Wilbur
Winner: Rose Kelleher, *Bundle o' Tinder*

2008
Judge: Alan Shapiro
Winner: Carrie Jerrell, *After the Revival*

For further information, please send an SASE to the press or go to the its website:

http://waywiser-press.com/hechtprize.html

A Note About the Author

Carrie Jerrell was born in Petersburg, Indiana, USA in 1976. She received her MA from the Writing Seminars at Johns Hopkins University and her PhD from Texas Tech University. A three-time Pushcart Prize nominee, she is an assistant professor of English at Murray State University in Murray, Kentucky and serves as the poetry editor for *Iron Horse Literary Review*.

Other books from Waywiser

POETRY

Al Alvarez, *New & Selected Poems*
Robert Conquest: *Penultimata*
Morri Creech, *Field Knowledge*
Peter Dale, *One Another*
Erica Dawson, *Big-Eyed Afraid*
B. H. Fairchild, *The Art of the Lathe*
Jeffrey Harrison, *The Names of Things: New & Selected Poems*
Joseph Harrison, *Identity Theft*
Joseph Harrison, *Someone Else's Name*
Anthony Hecht, *Collected Later Poems*
Anthony Hecht, *The Darkness and the Light*
Rose Kelleher, *Bundle o' Tinder*
Dora Malech, *Shore Ordered Ocean*
Eric McHenry, *Potscrubber Lullabies*
Timothy Murphy, *Very Far North*
Ian Parks, *Shell Island*
Daniel Rifenburgh, *Advent*
W.D. Snodgrass: *Not for Specialists: New & Selected Poems**
Mark Strand, *Blizzard of One**
Bradford Gray Telford: *Perfect Hurt*
Cody Walker, *Shuffle and Breakdown*
Deborah Warren, *The Size of Happiness*
Clive Watkins, *Jigsaw*
Richard Wilbur, *Mayflies**
Richard Wilbur, *Collected Poems 1943-2004*
Norman Williams, *One Unblinking Eye*
Greg Williamson, *A Most Marvelous Piece of Luck*

FICTION

Gregory Heath, *The Entire Animal*
Matthew Yorke, *Chancing It*

ILLUSTRATED

Nicholas Garland, *I wish ...*

NON-FICTION

Neil Berry, *Articles of Faith: The Story of British Intellectual Journalism*
Mark Ford, *A Driftwood Altar: Essays and Reviews*
Richard Wollheim, *Germs: A Memoir of Childhood*

*Expanded UK edition